Also by Stephen Oliver

Henwise
& interviews
Autumn Songs
Letter To James K. Baxter
Earthbound Mirrors
Guardians, Not Angels
Islands of Wilderness—A Romance
Unmanned
Election Year Blues
Night of Warehouses: Poems 1978-2000
Deadly Pollen
Ballads, Satire & Salt—A Book of Diversions
Either Side The Horizon
Parable Of The Sea Sponge
Harmonic
Apocrypha
Intercolonial

GONE

SATIRICAL POEMS: *NEW & SELECTED*
Stephen Oliver

Illustrated by Matt Ottley

GP
GREYWACKE PRESS
Lat. 25°/50° South. Long. 145°/180° East

First Published 2016

Greywacke Press
9 Lynch St
Hughes
ACT 2605
Australia
tasvagantes@gmail.com

Oliver, Stephen, 1950-
ISBN 978-0-473-36004-7
Title: GONE

Cover Design: Stephen Oliver

Cover image: *Gasworks In Chelsea*, 2nd composition, on the back of an envelope, by Alfred Francis Griffen, September 1935.

© Stephen Oliver

All rights reserved.
No part of this publication may be reproduced, stored in a retrieval system, or transmitted in any form or by any means, electronic, mechanical, photocopying, scanning, recording or otherwise, without the prior permission of the copyright owner.

DEDICATED
to the memory of
Warren Dibble 1931-2014
playwright, poet, friend

Acknowledgements

A number of the new poems first appeared in: *Antipodes: A Global Journal of Australian and New Zealand Literature* (Australia / USA); *broadsheet nos 1 / 16* (NZ); *New Zealand Listener; Poetry Wall Anthology* (NZ); *Sterz* (Austria).

Ballad of Elsie Brooks subsequently appeared in *Apocrypha* by Stephen Oliver, Cold Hub Press, Governor's Bay, NZ, 2010.

My thanks to Dr. Heinz Leonhard (Leo) Kretzenbacher, German Studies, School of Languages and Linguistics, the University of Melbourne, who translated into German the poem *Bad Aussee*.

Poems (including original notes and illustrations) are taken from *Ballads, Satire & Salt – A Book of Diversions*, Greywacke Press, Sydney, 2003. Illustrations are by Matt Ottley who supplied additional drawings for *Ballad Of A Yobbo* in the *New Poems* of this book. See *Notes* section.

My thanks to David Walker, Local Studies Librarian at the Kensington Central Library, London, where the Alfred Francis Griffen Collection is held, for generously allowing me to reproduce the watercolour sketch, *Gasworks In Chelsea*.

Gaudeamus Igitur and *Ballad of Miss Goodbar* recorded by the author with original music by Matt Ottley, KING HIT CD, Interactive Digital, Brisbane, 2007.

My especial thanks to Nicholas Reid of Canberra and John Denny of Puriri Press, Auckland, for assistance in preparing this book.

Contents

Ballad Of Miss Goodbar	3
Dylan Thomas	5
Mururoa Truffles	6
Ballade of A Glossy	8
You See The Anthology Man	10
Philip Larkin, Recalled	11
W. H. Auden	13
Sydney Bells	14
Tupícya	17
Heaven	19
Our Lady Of The Anthropologists	20
Letter To James K. Baxter	22
The Lover	32
Song Of The Trades	33
Uncle Ben	36
Legerdemain	37
'Living Forever'	38
Doctor Rock	39
Miss Lily	40
Gaudeamus Igitur	46
Ballad Of The Taj Mahal	47
Greatness	49

New Poems

Swagman's Song	53
Fridge Cat	54
Ballade Of The Poster	56
Bad Aussee	58
Of Poets & Peddlers	60
Verse Lightly	62
Ballad of A Yobbo	63
Psychosis	67
The Gesture	68
Gone	69
'The Lost Hurrah!'	71

Seraphic Creatures	72
No One Knows	73
Blockbuster Ode	74
Poetry Day Blues	75
Ballad of Elsie Brooks	76
Night	78
Notes	*i-vii*

GONE

BALLAD OF MISS GOODBAR

Miss Goodbar did bondage to the two-backed beast
with a body decked out like a picnic feast;
turned a few smart tricks every night at least,
    she prayed would last forever.

The neighbours they lamented the noise she made,
and petitioned to get that good lady spayed;
we've all got a particular stock and trade,
    who believe love lasts forever.

They took that petition to the councillor
and rapped loud and long upon his redwood door,
didn't hear him screwing on the parquet floor—
    the world spins on forever.

The weekend rolled on, and the weekend rolled by,
for Janitor Jock had a wandering eye;
slipped on his sneakers and buttoned up his fly,
    whose soul shall burn forever.

Late Sunday night about ten it must have been
not a creature stirred except the streetwise queen—
issued from Miss Goodbar's pad a high pitched scream,
    that echoed on forever.

They called in the coppers with guns on the hips,
they called in the priest with a prayer on his lips;
they dusted down Miss Goodbar for finger-prints—
    and a bed gone cold forever.

Next to her body lay a bunch of brass keys,
not what you'd expect to be the normal fees;
was slit wide open from her neck to her knees—
    the blood flowed on forever.

They took Jock away and they gave him a trial,
then tied him to a chair and fried him awhile—
yet no-one could account for that wayward smile,
    frozen on his face forever.

Her first great lover was Christ upon the Cross,
her second-rate lover, an insurance boss—
Miss Goodbar lies tucked in a bed of green moss,
    and there she sleeps forever.

DYLAN THOMAS

A frothy moon and planets wagon deep
as lights slowly lifted on Brown's Hotel
and Dylan leaning there over an ale,
eyes black as coal from an eternal sleep.

'Listen,' he said, 'Some soberly advice,
heavy liquor's for the screaming banshees
avoid the depth charge of double whiskies,
essentially, it's a matter of price.'

The vision faded out to closing time
and the hours peddled a bike down the lane,
the sound of glasses and talk receded.

Awakened now by warblings of a plane
through embankments of cloud into sunshine,
I thought of his tours, how Caitlin pleaded.

MURUROA TRUFFLES

(*après moi le déluge*)

O France's Gaullist government
   of President Chirac
has made it clear to us down here
   nuclear testing's back—

'don't doubt I plan to detonate
   there's nothing you can do,
when deep beneath Mururoa
   I set a bright flambeau.

'In the sea depths of the basalt
   under the coral cone,
I'll boil *bombe à la fricassee*
   within a pot of stone.

'Elite commandos in dinghies
   do ceaselessly patrol
round the 12-mile exclusion zone,
   round that *petit-atoll*.

'We bombed the *Rainbow Warrior*
   our frogmen played the prank
in Auckland harbour blew her hull,
   and so it was she sank.

'We are a force upon the earth
   and Greenpeace contests it.
France I say is here to stay in
   case you hadn't guessed it.

'O France's pride is paramount
   therefore I do no wrong,
don't doubt I plan to detonate
   Vive la bombe! Vive la bombe!'

France fell before the Boche's boot
   which made of her a whore,
Chirac's the New Napoleon
   he's on the march once more.

BALLADE OF A GLOSSY

In trains by Pymble and Central Station,
in lifts from the first to the second floor,
in brick bungalows throughout the nation,
one can't imagine what they did it for,
in fact, behind every fly-screen door,
in cattle pens of the dry Kimberley
women would snicker, sneer, chuckle and roar
and read the *Australian Women's Weekly*.

Our mothers devoured it with a passion
between baking and the latest league score,
what the queen said, who promoted fashion,
did Cary Grant inseminate that whore,
was Grace Kelly upset by a cold sore?
While the winds of change blew but meekly
women pickled and stewed, knuckled and swore
and read the *Australian Women's Weekly*.

To each appetite its daily ration
of sex, beauty, youth and a touch of gore,
the nun, the mutant, the sex-slave Martian,
more lies please, it's the truth I abhor.
Whatever the next issue holds in store
it will help to break the monotony
as I scrub and iron and chop and snore
and read the *Australian Women's Weekly*.

Envoy

Now if you contend that life's a bore
pause for a glass of dry, chilled Chianti
to toast Our Lady of Domestic Law,
and read the *Australian Women's Weekly*.

YOU SEE THE ANTHOLOGY MAN

I am you see the anthology man,
very much the fashion, and so today,
I will let you into my little plan.

I adopt a style to seduce the fan;
(one feels *freed* in a familiar way)
I am you see the anthology man.

I shift with fashion, a chameleon,
the man for all seasons, and so today,
I will let you into my little plan.

I am a poseur but of marked *élan;*
(as the ego-gathering tides hold sway)
I am you see the anthology man.

A solipsist does whatever he can,
the devil take the rest, and so today,
I will let you into my little plan.

Any talent challenging me I ban;
(mine is an *exclusive brand* of poesy)
am I you see the anthology man?
I will let you into my little plan.

PHILIP LARKIN, RECALLED

Dear PHILIP, take this as update
on much you've missed in being late,
you stepped out around '85
then took off for your longest drive,
away down nut-strewn lanes you went
without a passport or a cent
and, that was that, I lamented,
now I'm left with your *Collected*.

This is a newsletter of sorts
just a few light-hearted reports,
I trust you're not easily bored—
on events both here and abroad;
I read of some chapel burnt down
in Suffolk it was, but what town ...
(without a doubt, medieval—
made the front page of *The Beagle*.)
Of this you would not wish to hear
for it could only bring a tear
to your sad, celestial eye;
PHILIP, I'm writing to say, Hi!
Your beloved country fares poorly,
right now she needs a Robin Hood
of poesy for the Common Good
to give back to the people what
post-modern poets have not got:
your fine, light touch, discipline too,
feet on the ground and a world view:
Britain lost the Thatcher wager—
(before Blair, it went to Major.)
Who's winning the poetic stakes?
I don't think any from— 'The Lakes',

but one they call John Ashbery
which you said rhymed with raspberry;
what other news can I give you,
the pill's still around, women too,
though AIDS has taken out a few.

A brick, a sport, a fine fellow,
here's to you at your High Window.

W.H. AUDEN

Always giving the aerial picture
of the age in which you lived, the odd war
(for this a trip to Iceland served as cure)
your face became the map of metaphor.

Yours pals Spender, MacNeice and Isherwood
agreed that a weed was far too pretty
while the gas-tank held the Platonic Good;
beauty you assessed as cause for pity.

Now the Berlin Wall has come tumbling down
and neo-fascist youth is on the rise;
many as gorgeous as the boys you knew.

Narcissus has taken a new disguise
with refugees flooding every town,
that Europe is a mess wouldn't shock you.

SYDNEY BELLS

Gays go up and gays go down
to ring the bells of Sydney town.

Suspenders and tarts,
say the bells of St Mark's.

Zip up your flies,
say the bells at St Ive's.

Pants full of piles,
say the bells at St Giles'.

No worries mate,
say the bells at Ramsgate.

No drinks to minors,
say the bells of Maria Regina's.

Pots of old paints,
say the bells of All Saints.

A joint and champagne,
say the bells at Balmain.

Politicians and hat tricks,
say the bells at St Patrick's.

Sausages in batter,
say the bells at Parramatta.

Bimbos bring hassles,
say the bells of St Basil's.

A turd in your eye,
say the bright bells at Bondi.

I've got a court date,
say the bells at Mortlake.

Marriage banns?
say the bells of St Anne's.

Can't pay my tax fee,
bang the bells at Bexley.

Go broke on *New Start*,
loll the Bells of Leichhardt.

Who's at the door?
say the bells at Enmore.

Here comes a taxi to take you home,
and here comes a train to grind you to bone.

TUPÍCYA

(*for Erin*)

When monkeys chewed baccy
and the forests glared lime-green,
when rivers ran backwards
and the trains ran out of steam

the people of *Tupícya* on
floating islands sailed off-shore
the inland seas and waterways as
they'd often done before;

to catch a Tupícya bird
who lays one egg twice a year,
round and black as a cannon ball
which many claim is square.

O the Tupícya bird rudely
bellows mad as a Brahmin bull,
flashes its yellow tail-feathers
with a curious mating call.

It echoes under rushlight
by the coast of the China Sea,
it echoes from the barren steppe
by the ancient ginkgo tree.

To get to Tupícya country
by bus or steamboat's tricky too,
and never go by very fast car
or you'll simply miss the view:

travel the old trade route
from Xian via The Nanjing Way,
and don't forget an overnight bag
for the skies are loud and grey.

HEAVEN

Heard about it before but where?
no way rocket ships can get there.
A thought can't and a thought is free
though requires far less energy.
We are caught between the devil
and deep desire for space travel.
A swallowing of all that light
and no sign of life, it's not right.
Surely we would have heard by now.
The Ancients often held powwow
with the gods—yet *they* believed it!
History played the slickest trick
when Heaven starred as city-state.
(Popes tried it on, but much too late).
Gravity pulls us back to earth,
something to do with human worth.

If God in his high Heaven blinks
you hear him gargle in your sinks,
when solar winds emit a groan
knocking out your cellular phone
or stopping lifts between the floors
(we spend half a life trapped indoors)
when magnetic storms play havoc
and Wall Street bulls start the panic,
or the godwit flies left to right
scrambling for its seasonal flight
and crows fly backwards in chevron
from Mullumbimby to Darwin—
whisper into your neighbour's ear
what one poet sang in Good Cheer
(never the one to scrimp and save)
'Each day's a holiday from the grave'.

OUR LADY OF THE ANTHROPOLOGISTS

O I think hers a modern
mind, stand up for Katerina,
whose thought is not diminutive
like the *anthropoidea;*

delicate as an artefact
she lectures on a little fee
the computations (and the graph)
of Polynesian pottery.

Information catalogued
(singly) anthropological,
the sherds, shells and coprolites
in the Pacific Triangle

confound her noble colleagues
each of whom propounds his claim:
what made ancient tribes run round,
was it sunshine, was it rain?

Professor Cant, the hierophant,
pegs a square of blue-vein cheese
contends that pre-historic man
did not recline on bended knees

but being a biped, naturally,
walked at first upon his feet
and just before his class at four,
swallows down a piece of meat.

Within that white lecture room
the ventilation softly hums
which students have deciphered as
the thrumming of the tribal drums.

O Katerina's rounded thigh
to touch, is strictly forbidden,
for what concerns the professor
is moa bone and the midden.

LETTER TO JAMES K. BAXTER

(An Old Hippie's last trip down the Yellow Brick Road)

Man (you're coming across!) I see you
   shamble at a tangent, an ill-dressed shade
heading down to the river, a hairy Esau,
   where Charon is waiting to have you weighed
   to dump your pack, chuck costume aside—
the loosely tied dogma, the pet philosophies
and all the gear made for the mind to tease,

to wrap—made to turn on the status quo.
   Man, across this other side of the border
I throw out my best wishes to the tow
   and for the trip, while time idles, this letter
   to browse as you shift topside for a breather,
knowing the deck hands for a morose mob
without the prospects and without the job.

As distance diminishes Charon's boat
   and the pilot light burns red on the mast,
and the bollard trails on the waters a rope ...
   Once, twice, the chant for somebody missed:
   heart-dead in Auckland: you answered.
Well, ferrying doesn't turn me on (I fly)
if the Cook Strait is anything to go by.

Rain overhead, and that reminds me—
   an acre of roof to tar, brush and paint
in the few week days left that are sunny.
   Far out, I'll trust to luck my patron saint
   till the weather shows some sign of restraint;
the hour moves on, I've a busy schedule,
I scratch on my sleeve: LOVE IS PRACTICAL.

A jaunt by boat that isn't headed far,
   two or three hours at most ... and a sunset.
likewise, five minutes on a cable car
   is about as much as I'm prepared to take.
   And walking (the risk of arriving late)
is, above all, the way I take my travel;
or that's how I grooved when I was single.

Married now, I'm given over to the itch
   for travel, for the foreign scenery,
tossing for a change we bought two tickets
   left the *Black Swans of Pauatahanui*
   (we rented a shack there) chose the red clay,
the chillier climate, we moved south:
marriage as a gamble sometimes pays off.

2.

Hell is forever the season of Fall:
   each instant, a million souls burst aflame
as *The Omnipotent* deem them combustible,
   least, so that heavy, the fire-brand Calvin
   drummed in (the vibrations reached Dunedin)
hard to buy that those salamanders
burn, screech and sizzle like Lowell's spiders.

Hell is a tourist kick, a flag on the map
   set up by Christian control (not the AA).
The transport is hip, the climate is hot,
   enticements abound for the *emigre*
   as added incentive to the journey;
spectacular billboards boast the Good Life
that means no hardship, man, no nagging wife.

Hell is slick as any big business:
   marketing is sound, the budget's not mean
thanks to a well-briefed board of directors
   the company clubs and the research team,
     and, sure, the superannuation scheme.
Clients are taught (they pay a rip-off fee)
not all fishes come from the Holy See.

A bout of dirty weather up ahead—
   I'm pretty sure I heard a howling dog
the wind coming strong (he'll wake the dead)
   just where is it all at—and this fog! ...
     The boat, river, crew (and dog) obscured:
and that mist, thick as hallucination.
Maybe, man, hell is your destination?

3.

We pay our dues to the product well made:
   I observe your face scrawled on the mist-air
you're big business, your image has paid.
    Passing by a shop-front window I saw—
   and this vision put me on a downer ...
your face, impressed (bloodless) on a towel
a trendy / cotton / quasi / vernicle.

But don't get off on this rave of mine
   if I show how they're stealing your thunder
you're a commodity, you're big time,
    you've made it, you're a commercial number;
    yeah, I bet it grabs your sense of humour.
Though popular, I better let you know
you never sold fast as the Rev. Bob Lowe.

You (we know) made it with the apathetic
   the druggie, the dropout, the hippie
the lesbian, and, the alcoholic,
    the queer and the (could I call you Hemi?)
    You had an ear for Everyman's story.
Too bad you didn't get time to hear mine.
I'll add that to the letter in a later rhyme.

You're added like a fact to our nation
   by which I mean the corporate image,
so you get, man, a standing ovation
    giving rise to the thing: CONSCIOUSNESS.
    By a cool twist of metamorphosis
you became the body and blood of a metaphor—
we don't knock it, it was you held the floor.

A people—we just haven't the stability
   that flows by the banks of time and custom;
the hourly news teaches us our history.
   What's not practical equals a big yawn;
   DIY pretty much is rule of thumb.
We don't own a national saint—but cheer
that oddball: the *Sportsman of the Year*.

Wasn't it Glover said at your wake—
   it wouldn't be long before they gave you
the rank that will set you up as a saint?
   No King George Medal, no Olive Laurel,
   just beatitudes and a plastic halo:
Campbell didn't trust you with his women
till you creek-jumped to Catholicism.

Yet I don't want to blow your trip,
   certainly don't want to be, *ah,* pharisaical;
even as your corporeal light (dig it)
   dims to dust and I warm to a parable
   we hear the priest grooving on a moral.
Meantime, the apologists are freaked for fun:
God / Man / Poet? Maybe all three in one?

The *Big Stone of Respectability*
   blocks us in, it's a mountain to be moved.
Some few have the strength and agility,
   fewer still know where to find a handhold.
   You shoved it free and tightened the blindfold,
put on a sheepskin (maybe gabardine?)
You walked that plank across the lion's den.

And, *so what!* if you were messianic:
   but never extreme, man, never militant,
though if it rose on the mind-graph: panic:
   you flogged it back with a buckle-belt
   the stinging reminder given with each welt...
you weren't Christ. Who was that Irishman
wrapped himself in chains to do the same?

4.

Now it's autumn. Under the shadow
   the garden craps out (no hope for the corn)
I study the hedge and watch the holes grow...
   my son drags his wooden-bee on the lawn.
   Yeah man, remember that ancient scene
when I showed you my first funky sonnets:
ornate as old dames in flowery bonnets.

Enclosed is a pic. of where we're living;
   hope it isn't crumpled in the mail,
in the foreground grows the *hedge-in-a-ring*.
   Uterine: but on a much larger scale;
   get the focus, it's not too bad at all!
To the left out of view stands the tannery;
owning your own shack—that means money.

Let me take a trip back to childhood:
   to slow up the frames, point out the scene
on how I inched up (don't mean babyhood)
   the infant in his exultant Eden—
   too much footage for this introduction;
I'll skip the scene of the catapult club
or how I plumbed manhood inside a pub.

Example: two quick flashes come to light
   grandpa Lou's *artificial foot* in a cupboard,
when he died, mother kept it by right ...
   the family held things ... they used to hoard.
   Instance: biscuits decayed in tins long stored.
I remember, too, when someone's mongrel
broached the hencoop, shredded every fowl.

I soon clicked "Life" ran to a new rule—
   something shifted, freed long frozen locks,
I began to turn on, to use my cool;
   pre-puberty-pink and lime green socks!
   The mid-fifties had me by the bollocks.
Coolly slipping between the parent and state,
pop culture became my new playmate.

I came on the tail end of Haley's Comets,
   Rock 'n' Roll (tree-fort days and a rope swing!)
Can't have been much more than five or six.
   Not long after, came beatniks and brylcreem,
   after the craze died on Johnny Devlin.
Between times I read a heap of Zane Grey;
I dream the purple sage to this very day.

With slick kiss-curl my eldest brother
   kept right up on the hottest of the rock,
the radio with built-in record player
   spun the plastic platters of the *top pop:*
   Buddy Holly, Fabian (but he was a flop).
Then came that dynamo of pelvic energy,
the Great King of Rock 'n' Roll: Elvis Presley.

Didn't have any quiet upbringing—
    four brothers and a sister made competition
one hell-of-a-lot more bitching than singing,
    so I took up with the music revolution
    to find an emotional Plimsoll line ...
learning to daydream in an electronic noise,
that became one of my favourite ploys.

5.

Yo! Interactive communication:
    a world hard-wired to the DJ patter,
the satellite, the transmitter station—
    (way before the world of email chatter)
    succinct as any play by Pinter;
our condition—I don't mean to be heavy,
remains that of a scrambled sensibility.

Don't get the idea I'm out of my head
    sending up this game, the age we live in,
(*stuff it!* where we lie we make our bed)
    can't get off on the Great Illumination—
    like tuning in to the days of Marsden,
can't charter discoveries like one poet;
exhilaration won't fire from my musket!

Illumination? The poet's got to act:
    so he decides to give identity,
to our small history, spiritual fact.
    He sets caulking a poem on discovery
    to build an ark for New Zealand Poetry.
One temptation we should deny ourselves
is to reach for bickie tins on high shelves.

Before I get onto art and all that,
   I'll move on to sketch the community
of youth, and about where my story's at,
   (on my list this gets top priority)
   in the section marked: Autobiography.
I must have stopped growing some years ago,
I'm still about 5'6" from head-to-toe.

O to escape the great urban sprawl—
   away from the paranoia of conurbation;
I still remember as a kid at school
   walking hills now boxed in sub-division—
   who can ramble a quarter acre section?
Within a month you'd see a new smoke stack
turn the sky dirty as a shook coal sack.

Wellington: 'city of the soulless'
   or so you reckoned, too bad, I think of
buildings high as wheat on those husky hills
   as a stamping ground, as my home city ...
   a scene you knocked about as a postie.
I packed up my books and pots, greased the car
and one bleak hour split on the *Aramoana*.

6.

The '60s announced open house:
   in city and suburb the word then spreading
to the lost and fallen and unloved youth.
   Dribs to droves meant columns migrating—
   this was the start, the age of communing;
press and parent couldn't bring back children
who flocked to your call: *Jerusalem!*

Then the pseudo spiritualism hit:
   all things eastern: Krishna, Buddha and Zen,
Jesus freaks mobilised aboard a truck;
   home spun neo-existentialism—
   how to exorcise that incubus, Time.
Sure enough, the emotion went out of it;
from those ashes cheers the New Socialite.

Anyway, I escaped it. You could say
   I didn't turn myself onto that game—
socially. I was uncool, I was shy;
   sternly taught to greet folk by surname,
   note my style yet retains a formal stain.
Right on! it didn't take long for novelty
to roll the joint of respectability.

What did it man? The sun taper thin
   calling you from autumn Dunedin, or
leaves thick as manuscripts in the Octagon.
   Maybe some hassle, some domestic law—
   promptings that pushed you out the door?
Groovy—how I'd dig to do that, a gas
to leave behind me my *bourgeois* shit house.

PS:

I spun out. The house? that's behind me,
   garden, wife, the kid, and all the rest.
I headed North again to hit the home city
   with a bumper load of books (only the best).
How many Steads can fit in a tea-chest?
That's how it went man, I left real quick. *Yeah!*
with HARDY, CHAUCER, THE BIBLE, SHAKESPEARE.

THE LOVER

A touch of charm and total attention
was one device which assured his success
with women though he tended to excess;
those over forty don't rate a mention.

Although he considered the kiss a bore
the flash cars and *Glenfiddich* did the trick;
generous to a fault, tacky and slick,
he sought in each the virgin and the whore.

His love was as abstract as fantasy:
the preceding lovers and how they screwed,
we assume he dredged the female psyche.

Yet all of them outgrew him by a feud;
after the parties and pornography
they found him sad and obvious—not lewd.

SONG OF THE TRADES

        1.

    Sang the wharfie
to the migrant from a foreign land,
I've Dutch clogs & clews by the container load
with a year's supply of contraband,
    by the harbour lights
    beside the slippery sea.

        2.

    Sang the bhagi
holding aloft the Golden Koran,
I would float up to heaven more quick I know
booking P & O package tour plan,
    by the harbour lights
    beside the slippery sea.

        3.

    Sang the prawnie
out of Cooktown on the turning tide,
I've trawled for eel & shark & the Balmain bug
O Dockside Suzie she's got it fried,
    by the harbour lights
    beside the slippery sea.

4.

Sang the smithy
as his hammer rang about the roof,
I've dry-shod bays & brumbies but I'd prefer
the waves that dance with a cloven hoof,
> *by the harbour lights*
> *beside the slippery sea.*

5.

Sang the firey
from Jannali down to Lovett Bay,
I've battled bushfires & firestorms hours on end
though arsonists I'd torch one a day,
> *by the harbour lights*
> *beside the slippery sea.*

6.

Sang the hippy
in Fitzroy on Brunswick's busy street,
a mind-fuck's my thing & women are my prey
I'm an old grey-tail who likes his meat,
> *by the harbour lights*
> *beside the slippery sea.*

7.

Sang the poli
in Canberra on a winter's night,
native title or land claims we frame the laws
the matter is simply black & white,
> *by the harbour lights*
> *beside the slippery sea.*

8.

    Sang the deckie
on the container—*Geiho Maru,*
I've seen St. Elmo's Fire frap from stem to stern
and dolphins herd fish as cowboys do,
    by the harbour lights
    beside the slippery sea.

UNCLE BEN

It came as a dumb shock to me
   when aged round about five or six
that bending down behind a bush,
   he said he had some other tricks
      Uncle Ben's bare bottom.

To me he seemed the funny man
   it really gave me quite a fright,
though I got toys and other things
   this looked so female fat and white
      Uncle Ben's bare bottom.

Was this a secret to be kept?
   kids are cruel we know is true,
of course I ran bawling to tell
   how I was forced to stand and view
      Uncle Ben's bare bottom.

Oh, sundry excuses were made,
   low mumblings parents are good at
designed to put the child at ease;
   they closed the subject after that
      Uncle Ben's bare bottom.

As stars goose-bump onto the sky
   and the moon floods over the land,
look to the bright constellations
   and there mapped in God's right hand
      Uncle Ben's bare bottom.

LEGERDEMAIN

It would be sacrilege to seek
   a clean place on the world map,
for you'd be walking forever
    from death to your birth and back.

Sex is the great public secret
   which no one can believe in—
what's bargained for in pubs and clubs,
   neither more nor less than skin.

Television is our hearth-fire
   (a memory it is said)
and cars like wolves sneaky at night
   are visitors from the dead.

Every image that you've thought
   lived before you thought it through,
Freud is the sun and Jung the moon
   yet—the reverse may be true.

'LIVING FOREVER'

(*Human Genome Sciences are predicting
that by 2075 immortality will be a reality*
            - BBC documentary)

'*Oh dear, what fear! Oh bugger me!*
to live one hundred years, or three.

A living death, a deathless state,
to know forever—dreadful fate!

If *courage* became a mere chore,
would marriage be an endless bore?

To live forever—how unkind,
the triumph of the pagan mind!

Nowhere to run! no end in sight,
fate far worse than Sisyphus' plight:

that fabled slide into madness,
to know death, but not—in stasis;

A prisoner to the self's cell,
the heart one tocsin-tolling bell.

Nowhere to hide! Life as a God?
chasing one's tail—much like a dog.'

DOCTOR ROCK

(Sounding a sonnet for B.J & Associates)

He accumulated fans each new shift:
punk, reggae, indie, maybe some swamp rock,
pumped hip-hop and Motown and techno rift;
he timed the hits to the top of the clock—

while every other night of the week
sorted the hot-spots and the top-shelf tart:
and though he figured as the total freak
could work the women with a salesman's art.

Sexual conquests confirmed the cliché,
the white convertible, black top, the blonde
caught the marble-eyed gaze of the DJ;
without a doubt he felt that he belonged.

The cowboy: *Drifter on the fm Band?*
give him his due, the drugs and one night stand.

MISS LILY

(*for Matt Ottley*)

Let me tell an odd tale
   about Miss Eliza Lily,
she came from the western suburbs
   of a harbour-side city.

Miss Lily, *Dear Lady*—
   and Wacky, the cockatoo!
shared a drab, rickety mansion,
   (walled garden and outdoor loo).

By most considered short
   at fifteen hands from head to floor,
she measured in the order of:—
   let's say about five-foot-four.

One thing deserves mention
   like the ancient *Irish Elk* long dead
earned Miss Lily notoriety:—
   a pair of hands grew on her head.

A dab hand on the harpsichord
   she played the Bandicoot Serenade,
Wacky on the breadboard beat time
   and danced the harlequinade.

She'd pose as the shaggy moose
   that ambled round mountain lakes,
she hid out back in Huon-pine
   by the garden-shed and rakes.

Her fame grew increasingly,
   you might say by public pranks—
she'd take off to the oddest spots
   via bus-stops and taxi ranks.

In the Hilton Hotel foyer
   she'd often pose as a hatstand
freaking out the *maître d'hôtel*,
   next to the baby white grand.

She'd hike to the domain
   if the sky whipped up a storm,
she'd catch lightning bolts in her hand
   and hurl them about the lawn.

On Sundays she liked best
   to play ball on the Oval Green—
she used those hands to good effect
   as backstop to a baseball team.

The bus to Maggie's Market
   ran to time but the time ran slow;
Miss Lily counted red-brick villas
   by liver-brick row upon row.

Melons and muffins she picked
   enough to fill a wicker-basket,
Wacky meanwhile hissed and spat
   on cats at Maggie's Market.

Late at night she loved to jump
    and flap her hands as birds in flight,
under the lilac moon would sing
    delirious with delight.

Alert as a satellite dish
    the hands sprouting on her head;
the dolphin and the dugong sang
    lullabies to her in bed.

O Miss Lily's golden hair
    glowed fiery in the setting sun,
she shared the secrets of the forests
    with boys and girls just for fun.

She told them of medicines
    in rainforests under a curse,
she told them of bark and berries
    that cured Asian flu or worse.

She told them of rivers
    that flowed to a silver lagoon,
she told them of the far away seas
    that rolled to the lilac moon.

One night the sky grew dark
    then black and even blacker still,
Miss Lily sent the children home
    as the wind blew loud and shrill.

It howled on into the night
    and the steeple-bells rang madly,
it knocked chimney-pots into streets
    and behaved very badly.

High up on Mt Wellington
    pylon cables came crashing down;
the one sole source of energy
    in that storm-tossed harbour town.

They called out civil defence
    who considered themselves the best,
they even called out the bowling club
    who woefully proved a pest.

The town mayor threw a fit
    and the councillors heaved a sob,
the townsfolk had enough and cried:
    PUT MISS LILY ON THE JOB!

She took the broken cables—
    clenched them in both her hands,
she fused the cable-ends together
    where the lonely pylon stands.

She lit up like some beacon
    much brighter than a movie star,
household lights came streaming on
    and the mayor shouted the bar.

So by public vote all agreed:
    ERECT A STATUE OF MISS LILY.
If she considered this *déclassé*
    Wacky didn't think it silly.

In the gallery she now stands,
    a sandstone slab in the Great Hall:
her hands clasped above her head
    next to the wombat Big as a Bull.

GAUDEAMUS IGITUR

Billy and his babe, armed, up on the roof,
appears at this distance, well—quite aloof;
one bullet drills headmaster through the eye,
his gown flutters, he flops like a magpie.
She cocks one leg like a stork and giggles,
puts a hand on her hip, pouts and wiggles;
*'Oh, neat one Billy! another dead bod,
I say, there's quite a pile down in the quad.'*
Matron by the oak, dashes for the door,
too late!—her tartan skirt splattered in gore.
That fat kid, bailed up, holding in his tum,
is gut-shot, why he's screaming for his mum.
The chaplain holds up his crucifix, begs
them to stop, but cops one between the legs.
Billy dreams he's in a computer game
against his will and every day's the same;
enough! enough! enough! enough! enough!
he has no future, couldn't give a stuff—
gets a head in his sights, sees it explode;
takes the girl from behind and blows his load.
This is the world then, what it has become;
therefore, let us rejoice—evil's great fun!

BALLAD OF THE TAJ MAHAL

A restaurant with fountain and water-clock
comprised one plan for a shut down toilet block—
domed like a mosque, chained, under padlock;
    enshrined as the Taj Mahal.

Years long and rusty this privy stood disused,
many a gland, they say, was here defused;
such gentlemen taken short were not amused—
    preyed on at the Taj Mahal.

Came here the councillors plans to invent,
they prayed that success would be heaven sent;
but know their bowels were as thrifty as lent,
    squatting in the Taj Mahal.

The saturated walls soon gave short shrift
to new laid plans when the precincts were sniffed—
many shed a tear over schemes gone adrift,
    to jazz up the Taj Mahal.

A smart Greek suggested a drive-in car wash,
so why go down-market when you can go posh?
It's all one to derros—they don't give a toss,
    pissing on the Taj Mahal.

Oh, the writing, it's certain, was on the wall,
though not all such sentiments were shared by all—
still, drains will gurgle after heavy rainfall,
    in troughs by the Taj Mahal.

If the walls of Jericho fell to the trumpet;
know that these will stand or fall on their merit,
no matter what gay boy sets out to mourn it—
      lost days at the Taj Mahal.

Some dream of precious stones from far away,
some of amethyst, or onyx with pearl inlay,
some of greenstone from down Hokitika way;
      to brighten the Taj Mahal.

If fire engines scream, and the traffic roars by,
and walls have ears, though you cannot guess why—
take a glass of chablis beneath a domed sky,
      to salute the Taj Mahal.

GREATNESS

This is our first understanding of loss,
it rises up before you through jungle
where sky turns the colour of verdigris,
it invokes the half-bad dreams that rankle.

What manifests is slowly surprising
as if you had suspected the image;
a train's ghostly beam in fog emerging,
the light molten, a river-spanning bridge.

What comes after anticipates vision,
for the mind that opens out will amaze—
how much is trusted, what hangs in balance.

As truth is perception that ricochets
off stonework in some cataclysmic dance
of all that went before now arisen.

NEW POEMS

SWAGMAN'S SONG

(Concerning the author, Bob Orr, and a glass door)

A beer and a yarn with an old mate
    is friendship's most basic law,
you might arrive early, or might arrive late,
    but watch out for Bob Orr's glass door.

Whiskey's a thing I avoid like the plague,
    it lays me out flat on the floor,
you might get lucky, or you might get laid,
    but watch out for Bob Orr's glass door.

Poets and artists are a rummy breed,
    they take money from rich or poor,
stick to soup kitchens, enjoy the free feed,
    and watch out for Bob Orr's glass door.

FRIDGE CAT

(for Paul Sullivan)

So they call me the fridge cat,
but I am much more than that.
I balance the books, keep house,
no sight nor scent of a mouse.

My Master works a long day,
as I snooze the hours away.
On doorstep, the deck or ledge,
a warm spot under the hedge.

Though I can't run up a tree,
no cat gets the drop on me,
I preen, lick, comb and pamper,
long hair cats are so dapper.

The sunny days drift on by,
without haste I swat a fly.
I do more than just hang out,
Yo! Beware your local lout!

'Gin-ge', the bully-boy cat,
we fight, fur flies, bet on that!
The thug snuck across my lawn,
claws out for a stoush at dawn.

The Guardian at The Gate:
Master comes home after eight,
grabs himself a snack to eat,
and I get my chopped up meat.

I do sums, inside my head,
twelve-times-table before bed.
The fridge is my Shangri La,
my life and my guiding star.

Winter, a chilly wind blows,
then I warm my Master's toes.
The air is sharp, the moon high,
the fridge purrs and so do I.

BALLADE OF THE POSTER

Whatever event you wish to display,
on walls or billboards, any space at all,
posters to promote a movie or play,
some carnival, band, parade, or football;
on telegraph poles, bus stops, city mall,
posters on Main Street, in every café,
not forgetting the Community Hall,
and I think I'll go postering today!

Poster art arose under Jules Chéret,
in the Belle Époque, when as I recall,
Toulouse-Lautrec enjoyed *femme déclassée*,
a funny little man but no one's fool,
for his poster art was the best of all;
rain threatens, I'm ready for my foray
(I left my staple gun on a bar stool),
and I think I'll go postering today!

I've pasted all the way to San Jose,
I've pasted boulevards and City Hall,
I've pasted down by the Dock of the Bay,
I've pasted prairies and heard the call,
poster flora for the concrete jungle;
I was wild with a paste broom in my day,
still I abide by that one simple rule,
and I think I'll go postering today!

Envoy

Feel the bustle & hum the city pull,
the weather might turn so I won't delay,
I love the outdoors yet I hated school,
and I think I'll go postering today!

BAD AUSSEE

(for Jossy Gerö)

Yes, I remember Bad Aussee—
the name, because around midday,
mild and warm, the train shuffled in,
unhurriedly. It was mid-May.

Carriages squeaked. A girl giggled.
An alpine place, yet of some fame,
pretty chalets bunched together
made Bad Aussee—more than a name;

Arthur Schnitzler and Stefan Zweig,
Popper, Oskar Kokoschka, why—
there were many, Brahms and Mahler,
whose music must have filled the sky.

Others, Herbert von Karajan,
such ghosts, laughing, hung in the air
over mountains white as ice cream,
where I pined, there in Styria.

BAD AUSSEE

(für Jossy Gerö)

Ja, ich erinnere mich an Bad Aussee—
an diesen Namen! Es war gegen zwei,
ein milder Tag. Der Zug fuhr ein,
schön langsam. Es war Mitte Mai.

Waggone ächzten. Ein kicherndes Mädchen.
Ein Alpenstädtchen, doch mit Renommee,
hübsche Chalets, aneinander gedrängt:
mehr als ein Name ist dies Bad Aussee.

Arthur Schnitzler und Stefan Zweig,
Popper, Oskar Kokoschka, ja—
es waren viele dort, wie Brahms und Mahler,
deren Geigen ich im Himmel hängen sah.

Andere, wie Herbert von Karajan,
deren Geisterlachen die Luft verbarg,
hoch über den eiskremweißen Gipfeln,
auf die ich mich sehnte, dort in der Steiermark.

Translation: Heinz L. Kretzenbacher

OF POETS & PEDDLERS

(for Allan MacGillivray)

The laird in his castle spits at the night
and the sky turns sooty as bats take flight.
Waterfowl break cover out on the fen,
and laughter echoes loudly round the glen.
Warily, swaggering on the ramparts,
a broadsword in hand this curse he imparts:
'Who is it calls at this belated hour,
when the moon itself appears to glower?
Raise the portcullis, go piss in the moat!
grab the uninvited guest by the throat.
Yeoman! Unleash your bolt upon the foe,
God's my witness the devil lurks below!
Begone! Damned hobgoblin of a gilly,
for heaven's sake woman boil the billy.
Flashing lights! Alarums! Engines of war!
revelry, fists banging against my door—
some unwanted minstrel selling his lays
for a piece of bread—he's seen better days;
most likely seeking a goblet of wine,
or bed for the night, ignoring the sign:
Poets & Peddlers from this domain banned.
For whosoever sets foot on this land
shall feel the full fury of Culloden—
as my cudgel cracks open his noggin.
Be warned troubadour of the plaintive song,
I may not be right but am rarely wrong.'

'O relentlessly, a knock, knock, knocking
could be the hallway clock tick-tock ticking,
telling me dinner's about to be served.
(A glass of hock, lass, I'm feeling unnerved).
This insistent pounding. My rattled brain.

Feverish thoughts file past in ghostly train
like monks who chant in cloisters do—*too late,
too late*, the enemy stands at the gate!
Fire up the cauldron, pour the molten lead,
before my woman burns the bannock bread.
Hurl the bloated cattle, shovel the shit,
dig up the corpses and drain the cesspit.
Bury the gold hoard, deep, in a crock-pot,
rather death, I say, than forfeit that lot.

A curse on all poets—that wheedling breed,
bring me my armour and saddle my steed!'

VERSE LIGHTLY

How it got there no one really knows,
    spat out as if through some black hole,
a rent in the fabric of time that glows,
    a Chinese lantern hanging off a pole.

A bright ball that amounts to naught,
    'so this is what it means to be mortal.'
considered the orbiting astronaut,
    as he peered out through a glass portal.

BALLAD OF A YOBBO

Barry, dead keen on feral boar,
hunted that beast, then he killed it.
His .44 Magnum made the hit:
semi auto-action with a big bore.

He worked the circuit as stockman
up North, way back in his youth,
'what a great life that was—streuth!'
A good pair of boots and a fry pan.

Friday night's soak in the tub:
hair slicked back with old pig fat—
Barry donned a broad-brim hat,
and off he went to trash some pub.

On women he had a basic view
shared with mates by the stock pen:
'can't fuck 'em, chuck rocks at 'em'
he bluntly stated, stirring the stew.

Something spooked Barry lately,
was it the tucker or lumpy bed?
Something weird got into his head,
nightmares troubled him greatly.

First he blamed it on bad plonk,
he sank a few before hitting the sack
(a bottle of bourbon in his pack);
maybe he fancied a drunken bonk?

Demons had him by the balls—
it appeared he slowly decomposed;
this'll end badly, he supposed,
demons don't play Aussie rules.

Barry turned *Australopithecus:*
one cranky bloke on a short fuse,
years spent sculling the booze
sealed his fate with a deadly kiss.

His mates said it'd gone too far—
Barry collapsed in a bloody heap
as if hit by a road train in his sleep;
they sold him off to an abattoir.

Nightly, those gruesome dreams,
morphing into a pile of pig gut.
Shoveled into buckets onto a truck,
branded dog food on TV screens.

'Yobbomeat' stamped on the can,
'Tasty Tucker A Dog Loves To Eat'.
The Ads aired on Sesame Street,
a dog's best friend—Barry the man!

PSYCHOSIS

Starter motor, whirr of wings,
bird in the dead of night sings.
Gravel crunches under wheel,
engine steady, brakes of steel.

Glides softly by, barely heard,
thought it was a midnight bird.
Dark folds back to empty air,
distant & small, changes gear.

What goes ahead doubles back,
time stretches, time is a rack.
Stars are spark plugs in the night,
a thought by far surpasses light.

The child feels solitude vast,
and knows that this cannot last.
Recalls the loss with sadness,
and one short step to madness.

THE GESTURE

Lonely, he did his laundry late at night.
The churning song of the machine, you see,
was all that he needed for company—
lulled him to unsettled sleep, eased the fright.

Almost as though he suspected attack,
at what appointed hour he could not gauge.
Some recurrent dream, impotent, of rage,
as if something warned him to watch his back.

Friendly shrubs and trees encircled his place
that after sunset thickened to shadow;
like a crowd of people without a face.

The child he once was arose from below
who had he thought disappeared without trace,
and turning, gestured that he should follow.

GONE

Uncle Barny lived with us at our place.
For him the war was a bloody good show.
Yet though it all ended some time ago,
as the spitfire ace he made the skies safe.

Kettles shriek in every suburban house.
Someone plays an oboe in some back room
a half-forgotten, half remembered tune;
I hate my job, it croons, I hate my spouse.

The sun rolls westward on its rusty rim.
Dusk dulls into pewter. Streetlights come on.
From the radio drifts a winsome song—
the evening primrose, the lawns cut trim.

Next to the brickyard and misty canal
a school teacher peddles by lost in thought.
Carpet slippers, a pipe, one glass of port,
but a factory whistle breaks the spell.

Lanes fade off into countryside unseen.
Beyond city limits chugs one freight train.
At the last terrace and storm water drain
trucks crawl behind a hay baling machine.

It's better not to know what lies ahead.
We used to believe that the world was flat,
now belief in God seems pretty old hat.
Live for the moment is what Horace said.

Public Libraries everywhere shut down,
from Newcastle, Grimbsy, to Kensal Rise.
What with electronics, no big surprise—
it spreads like a virus from town to town.

Time accumulates like dust on a mat—
old gasworks by the tavern block the view,
a popular spot for the post-pub screw;
but in the end we grew quite sick of that.

'THE LOST HURRAH!'

A hard-bitten royalist's what I am,
    with pipe & port, and bedroom slippers.
I play up, play on, and I play the game,
    for Kipling O Kipling & fried kippers.

I'm an army brat from the Motherland,
    I swim ten lengths a day in pink flippers.
My wife ran away with Bob Dylan's band,
    for Kipling, O Kipling & fried kippers.

I collect old bottles from World War 1,
    bayonets, boots & rusty wire snippers;
I never got to kiss Rupert Brooke's bum,
    for Kipling, O Kipling & fried kippers.

SERAPHIC CREATURES

I

My name's Haldane of St Heliers,
recent convert to the Islamic State.
I grow gooseberries on espaliers,
and every day I pray 'God is Great!'

11.

I sell bulk chemicals to farmers,
on the freeway the earliest by eight.
I fancy small women in pajamas,
and every day I pray 'God is Great!'

111.

One spicy kebab and then to bed,
seraphic creatures protect my estate.
I horde fertilizer in my back shed,
and every day I pray 'God is Great!'

NO ONE KNOWS

No one knows what goes on inside my head,
one thought chases another one away;
least, that is what I think the Master said.

Some days I prefer to stay tucked in bed,
mood swings often as not take me that way:
no one knows what goes on inside my head.

Fear that erupts like gamma rays I dread;
such are those demons that lead one astray,
least, that is what I think the Master said.

One must work hard to keep the ego fed,
would that we were gods at the close of day:
no one knows what goes on inside my head.

That heavy footfall is the devil's tread,
quit the premises now—do not delay;
least, that is what I think the Master said.

You did not notice the neighours had fled
who disappeared before the break of day.
No one knows what goes on inside my head,
least, that is what I think the Master said.

BLOCKBUSTER ODE

We live in the Age of the Grand Cliché;
of viral beasts, vampires, it's their hay day.
Writers pour from the Iowa ramparts,
this is where the panic, the gold rush starts
for fellowships, stipends, and grants galore,
as publishers come banging on the door,
'give us mutants, gangsters, galactic sluts',
so writers sit to write on whorish butts
and hope against hope for the blockbuster;
poets on the other hand seem lacklustre.
Fame means ambition wedded to good luck,
really, that I should give a flying fuck.
Shakespeare's sonnets slyly debunked at last.
One Scottish poet thought it a real blast
to glibly dumb down the Swan of Avon;
(smug exercise at best, at worst craven).
This wheedling Calvin, this rheumy-eyed fop,
greasing his arse all the way to the top;
'against the stormy gusts of winter's day,'
serve him up his innards for Hogmanay!
Three cheers for Twitter and Facebook, iPod,
these have replaced the poet O poor sod!
Today the poem is product—a soufflé.
We live in the Age of the Grand Cliché.

POETRY DAY BLUES

So; let's wheel out the laureates
with ornately carved walking sticks,
Huey, Dewey, Dopey. Grumpy.
Yay! it's National Poetry Day.
Awards for faction and fiction,
for fancy post modern diction;
books on pies, and poems and puns.
Books on boats, bivouacs, and buns,
books about hubcaps, hiccups, bumps,
books on measles (the odd lumps).
There's the *Knife-In-The-Back Award*,
(I'm sure that's one I can't afford).
The senses spin, but what to choose?
That good ol' poetry lovin' blues.
Don't give up yet, oh, don't despair,
help is at hand for help is near.
Go ask *Snow White*—that babe knows
just which way the cool wind blows;
judge exemplar, queen of chick lit,
the rule-of-thumb *apparatchik*.
Poems about bagels, ladders, bikes,
poems praising porn, and Diesel Dykes.
Poems on pavements, poems on walls,
poems at bus stops, poems in halls.
The true (a few) the old, the fake,
a posse of poets—make or break.

BALLAD OF ELSIE BROOKS

Elsie Brooks! Oh, Elsie Brooks!
    The writer of children's books,
little heroes and heroines,
    always sunlit, free of sins.

Elsie Brooks! Oh, Elsie Brooks!
    The writer of children's books,
says greenies are the enemy,
    and worships at the money tree.

Elsie Brooks! Oh, Elsie Brooks!
    The writer of children's books,
hooks CEOs, inside traders,
    the well-hung, corporate raiders.

Elsie Brooks! Oh, Elsie Brooks!
    The writer of children's books,
is often found behind locked doors,
    spinning the bottle on all fours.

Elsie Brooks! Oh, Elsie Brooks!
    The writer of children's books,
ran away with the diplomat,
    he plucked car keys from a hat.

Elsie Brooks! Oh, Elsie Brooks!
    The writer of children's books,
is truth beauty and beauty truth
    in your Heaven of Hitler Youth?

Elsie Brooks! Oh, Elsie Brooks!
    The writer of children's books,
brown shirt & black lederhosen,
        proudly chanting *Blut und Boden*.

Elsie Brooks! Oh, Elsie Brooks!
    The writer of children's books,
not one of which was ever read,
        nobody cared now she's dead.

Elsie Brooks! Oh, Elsie Brooks!
    The writer of children's books,
little heroes and heroines,
        always sunlit, free of sins.

NIGHT

(*In a taxi between North Sydney and Kings Cross, pre-dawn*)

Opposite me two poets snore and fart,
  hurtling down the highway, pedal to floor.
A sordid night's jaunt in the name of art;
  one poet's a ponce, the other's a bore.
Against the graffiti wall leans a tart,
  the meter clicks over, keeping the score.
Our driver silent, still, playing his part.
  Opposite me two poets fart and snore....

One violently retches, soon settles down.
  Night coagulates, behind us the town
in the rear vision mirror, postcard size;
  harbour lights throw up another high rise.
Neon bluely fizzes, the night is raw....
  Opposite me two poets fart and snore.

NOTES

Notes

BALLAD OF MISS GOODBAR
Loosely based upon the 1977 movie, 'Looking for Mr Goodbar' starring Diane Keaton and Richard Gere.

Excellent examples of this form may be seen in Lawrence Durrell's 'A Ballad of The Good Lord Nelson' and James K. Baxter's 'Lament for Barney Flanagan'. The opening stanzas are:

Lawrence Durrell:

The Good Lord Nelson had a swollen gland,
Little of the Scripture did he understand
Till a woman lead him to the Promised Land
    Aboard the Victory, Victory O.

James K. Baxter:

Flanagan got up on a Saturday morning,
Pulled on his pants while the coffee was warming;
He didn't remember the doctor's warning,
    'Your heart's too big, Mr Flanagan.'

MURUROA TRUFFLES
The final six nuclear tests carried out in the South Pacific by the French government under President Chirac at the close of 1995 on Mururoa and Fangataufa atolls brought universal condemnation; the two largest of these underground detonations occurred on Fangataufa. France conducted 178 underground and atmospheric nuclear tests between 1966-1996. Recent surveys show crumbling and fractures at the base of these coral sites posing the threat of 'plutonium hot-spots'.

BALLADE OF A GLOSSY
Closely modelled on G. K. Chesterton's poem, 'Ballade of A Periodical' (a verse form he enjoyed and excelled in) found in the biography by Maisie Ward, *Gilbert Keith Chesterton*, Sheed & Ward, London, 1944, pp: 310-311. The first stanza runs:

In icy circles by the Behring Strait,
In moony jungles where the tigers roar,
In tropic isles where civil servants wait,
And wonder what the deuce they're waiting for,
In lonely lighthouses beyond the Nore,
In English country houses crammed with Jews,
Men still will study, spell, perpend and pore
And read the Illustrated London News.

SYDNEY BELLS
The line: *'Go broke on New Start'* is a bureaucratic euphemism for the Australian *Unemployment Benefit* commonly known as the Dole.

'Sydney Bells' is a passing tribute to one of the more endearing examples of the nonsense poetry genre; the anonymous nursery song, 'London Bells' which first appeared in *Tommy Thumb's Pretty Song Book* (c.1744) was published by the London Publisher, Mary Cooper. This collection is, by general agreement, the earliest known book of nursery rhymes.

The poem begins:

Gay go up, and gay go down,
To ring the bells of London town.

Bull's eyes and targets,
Say the bells of St Marg'ret's.

and ends:

Here comes a candle to light you to bed,
And here comes a chopper to chop off your head.

And then there is Idris Davies (1905-1953) born in Rhymney, Monmouthshire, a poet from the mining valleys of South Wales who spoke of the injustices and hardships suffered by the miners. Here's his *Gwalia Deserta* song:

O what can you give me?
Say the sad bells of Rhymney.

Is there hope for the future?
Cry the brown bells of Merthyr.

Who made the mineowner?
Say the black bells of Rhondda.

And who robbed the miner?
Cry the grim bells of Blaina.

They will plunder willy-nilly,
Say the bells of Caerphilly.

They have fangs, they have teeth!
Shout the loud bells of Neath.

To the south, things are sullen,
Say the pink bells of Brecon.

Even God is uneasy,
Say the moist bells of Swansea.

Put the vandals in court!
Cry the bells of Newport.

All would be well if-if-if-
Say the green bells of Cardiff.

Why so worried, sisters, why?
Sing the silver bells of Wye.

HEAVEN
The Wellington poet and satirist, Denis Glover, once quipped: *'Like all great fiction, I enjoy reading the Bible.'* He also said, *"Every day's a holiday away from the grave."* This took place during a 'live' television interview in the mid '60s. He was famously drunk at the time.

UNCLE BEN
Traumatic early memory, often manifest in adulthood, might have originated in simple trusts betrayed in the minds of children; this poem with its sinister undercurrent draws on one such 'incident' from early childhood. Uncle Ben was, typically, the nominal uncle— gift-bearer with the feather touch!

PHILIP LARKIN, RECALLED
I refer the reader to Larkin's poem for Charles Causley, 'Dear CHARLES, My Muse, asleep or dead' published in 'Poems for Charles Causley, 1982' and in PHILIP LARKIN, Collected Poems, edited with an introduction by Anthony Thwaite, Faber and Faber, 1988.

'you said rhymed with raspberry'
Philip Larkin, interviewed in the Paris Review (Summer 1982, No. 84) when asked if he would ever visit America, said: '... I'm so deaf now that I shouldn't dare. Someone would say, what about Ashbery, and I'd say, I'd prefer strawberry, that kind of thing. I suppose everyone has his own dream of America.' My 'raspberry' extends the jest.

MISS LILY
The Irish Elk (*Megaloceros giganteus*) had antlers spanning 3.6 to 4m and stood 2.10m at the shoulder. Existed up until about 9,200 years ago. Limited numbers survived the last Ice Age that stretched from 100,000 to 10,000 years ago. The Elk inhabited Ireland from 37,000 to 32,000 and again from 11,750 to 9,000 thousand years ago. The animal probably originated in Siberia and was not confined to Ireland. Remains have been found in Britain, France, Germany, Austria, Hungary, Northern Italy and Central Asia.

The *Diprotodon*, was the largest (wombat-like) marsupial that ever lived. This herbivore existed 1.6 million years until about 40,000 years ago. Measured 3m from head to toe, 2m tall at the shoulder. About the size of a hippopotamus. Another of the megafauna was the giant wombat: *Phascolonus gigas* about the size of the average Volkswagen. It died out at about the same time.

Miss Lily does not appear in fossil records.

GAUDEAMUS IGITUR
The title of this poem is taken from one of the oldest known European student songs, usually sung in the original Latin, as celebration of the 'free and easy student life'. The melody is notably famous as a German student drinking song from at least as early as the 17th century. Even today, many a middle aged German businessman will sentimentally recall *Gaudeamus Igitur* and the lost youth of his student days.

The melody first became popular through its inclusion in Akademische Festouvertüre for orchestra by Brahms, published in 1881. I would suggest to the reader that if he or she wants a Hollywood version of the song (not without its appeal) then Mario Lanza's rendition of the following verse from the 'Student Prince' is as rousing as any. Otherwise, I recommend the legendary Viennese baritone, *Erich Kunz: German University Songs, Vol. 1*. My poem is, therefore, to be seen within this context as reminiscent of '70s movies like 'If' and 'The Ruling Class'. A translation of the familiar, first verse from the Latin is as follows:

> *Gaudeamus igitur,*
> *Juvenes dum sumus;*
> *Post jucundam juventutem,*
> *Post molestam senectutem*
>   *Nos habebit humus.*

> *While we're young, let us rejoice.*
> *Singing out in gleeful tones;*
> *After youth's delightful frolic*
> *And old age (so melancholic!)*
>   *Earth will cover our bones.*

BALLAD OF THE TAJ MAHAL
The public toilet block known as the 'Taj Mahal' designed by architects of the Wellington City Engineering Office was built in 1928. The building's design is not without a certain, architectural humour; its curved north and south end walls, each capped with a dome, resemble that of a 'mosque'. This quasi-imperial style is listed on the *Heritage Inventory* as 'Inter War Free Classical'.

The edifice functioned as a WCC public toilet for forty years and finally closed in 1966. Fortunately, a strong public outcry saved the building from demolition. For about a decade it was used as storage space for nearby *Downstage theatre*. In 1978, after extensive renovations, the *Taj Mahal* reopened as an Art Gallery and Patisserie and became, latterly, a restaurant.

Environmental artists, Terry Archer and David Waterman, were commissioned to paint a fresco (Muldoon's visage peers troll-like from the puffy clouds) on the northern dome ceiling by the owner, Cynthia Cass, who bought the property in 1980. The building remains a significant cultural landmark, though continues to serve as a 'public bar' under shifting ownership and name.

FRIDGE CAT
Pastiche of the famous mediaeval poem *Pangur Ban* or *The Monk And His Cat* written about the 8th or 9th century in the margins of a psalter by an anonymous Irish Benedictine monk. He lived in the extant St. Paul's Monastery on Reichenau Island in Lake Constance (Bodensee) where Germany meets with Carinthia, Austria. Arguably, the best translation is by Robin Flower, renowned Celticist and translator of Tomás O'Crohan's *The Islandman*.

BALLADE OF A POSTER
The ballade made famous by François Villon originated in mediaeval and Renaissance French poetry. Chaucer was probably the first English poet to use the form. Ideally suited to satire, the ballade was much favoured by C.K. Chesterton and Hilaire Belloc. See note above on my earlier *Ballade of A Glossy* that first appeared in *Ballads, Satire & Salt—A Book of Diversions* illustrated by Matt Ottley (2003).

BAD AUSSEE
Modelled on Edward Thomas' better known *Adlestrop*. In May 1979, I visited Bad Aussee in Styria, Austria for a few days. The poem however, was written some three decades later. *Narzissenfest,,* Austria's biggest flower festival, is held every May-June in Bad Aussee when the daffodil (*narcissus poeticus*) is in full bloom and cloaks the alpine meadows.

OF POETS & PEDDLERS
Every thought is an act of translation: my rendering of an anonymous verse written on scraps of cowhide, probably by some disgruntled fellmonger, and found stuffed inside an old whiskey cask hidden in the wall of a schist, stack stone cottage near Bannockburn, Central Otago. The poem can be read as a Calvinistic imprecation against unwanted and uninvited guests. The language would suggest that the piece cannot be older than the late 19th Century.

BALLAD OF A YOBBO
Matt Ottley is an Australian children's picture book illustrator, graphic novelist, composer, and flamenco guitarist. *Requiem For A Beast* won the *Children's Book Council of Australia Picture Book of the Year* in 2008, and the *Queensland Premier's Award for Young Adult Literature* in

the same year. Matt Ottley and Rebecca Young won the *Patricia Wrightson Prize for Children's Literature* in the 2016 *NSW Premier's Awards* for *Teacup* (Scholastic Australia). 'Yob' describes someone who is 'rude, obnoxious, violent and stupid'. Truly, a *transtasman* aberration.

NIGHT
See Rupert Brooke's sonnet *Dawn* written in the early 1900s. There's an air of *fin de siècle* decadence about his poem. Brooke was, though not commonly recognized as such, a fine comedic poet. See his poem 'Heaven', for instance. He died of blood poisoning in the Dardanelles, April 23, 1915. He never saw active service. *Rupert Brooke—A Biography by Christopher Hassall*, first published by Faber and Faber in 1964, remains unquestionably the best biography on the poet ever written.

A NOTE ABOUT THE AUTHOR

Stephen Oliver—Australasian poet and author of 17 volumes of poetry. Travelled extensively. Signed on with the radio ship *The Voice of Peace* broadcasting in the Mediterranean out of Jaffa, Israel in the late 70s. Lived in Australia for 20 years. Currently living in NZ. He has published widely in international literary journals. Regular contributor of creative non-fiction and poems to *Antipodes: A Global Journal of Australian and New Zealand Literature*. Poems translated into German, Spanish, Chinese, and Russian. Represented most recently in: *Writing To The Wire Anthology*, edited by Dan Disney and Kit Kelen, University of Western Australia Publishing, 2016.

www.ingramcontent.com/pod-product-compliance
Lightning Source LLC
Chambersburg PA
CBHW021019090426